imeline ?

A Roman, Apicius, records the use of eggs in a recipe for baked custard. He omits the expletives he used when a fresh dozen landed on his baking-room floor.

25 B.C.

Coffee starts using the slogan, "Good to the last drop." Did Teddy Roosevelt say that while drinking at Nashville's Maxwell House Hotel? Only his teddy bear knows for sure.

1917

c. 1657

Coffee is a passion among Parisians. "The City of Light" takes it black.

@#$%!

breakfast

cock-a-doodle-do

breakfast

Eye-opening Fresh Flavors for
Before Your Eyes Are Really Open

By Beth Goehring

To Chuck and Grace:
You make it a joy to get up in the morning.

table of contents

introduction

Morning is the universe's way of saying, "Okay! Let's take it from the top." Each new day is another chance to get it right: to eat better, to plan smarter, to be nicer. Wash yesterday's sins away with a glass of cold orange juice or a pot of hot coffee. Let your first words be "I'm sorry," if need be, but say them with a smile and the promise to try harder next time.

This little book celebrates that promising moment before the bills arrive, you forget your umbrella, get a parking ticket or the dog eats your homework. Savor it. Don't stress about what to eat: make something you enjoy. Here are quick, easy and delicious ways to use fresh fruit, whole grains, some meat, veggies, leftovers, eggs, cheese and yogurt. There's little or no measuring required because you're not awake enough yet for all that fuss! It's a handful of this and a

introduction

smidgeon of that, plus inspiration from around the world, and simple advice to make your breakfast prettier and tastier. Before long, you'll enjoy throwing back your covers, heading to the kitchen and fueling up for the opportunity to start fresh.

Before we go, there is the question of whether or not to read the newspaper over breakfast. I cannot start my day without getting my fingers inky. For me, no website, however instant, pithy or opinionated in its presentation, can compare with the orderly progression of information a traditional newspaper offers. Do I cry over bad news? Oh, yes. Does that ruin my day? No. I feel more connected to my fellow travelers. If, however, the tragedies happening in the world affect you in such a way that breakfast isn't restful, do something else that inspires you. Doodle, chat on the phone, play with the kids or your pet. Or simply take the time to be in the moment and taste your breakfast. Think of it as a form of meditation where you quietly enjoy the first meal of the day and clear your mind to deal with what lies ahead. Life is too short to get all verklempt before 9 a.m.

As well as the time and inclination to kick-start a productive day, I hope you all have a wonderful cheerleader like my husband, Chuck, who sends me off to work each morning with a kiss and the instruction to "Knock 'em dead." He's there every evening, also, to bind up my wounds and listen to the war stories. It sure makes getting up the next day to do it all over again worthwhile.

why eat breakfast... and how

why eat breakfast...and how

I've never understood people who can't eat in the morning—I might as well go to bed with my apron on. Luckily, nutritionists back me up with a firm command to "Sit down and have a little something!" Without breakfast's calories, protein, fiber, vitamins and minerals, we can't focus, we'll be hungry and cranky by mid-morning and we'll be less healthy overall. It's vital to "break the fast" from the night before.

As with so much in life, the trick is to keep it simple. The ideas here are so easy; nothing except the pizza dough and the buttermilk pancake recipe requires measuring. Let me make myself perfectly clear: almost no measuring necessary.

These ideas call for a spoonful of this, a handful of that, a few sprinkles on top—you know your own tastes better than any cookbook writer. Whatever you eat, make it yourself from whole grains, fresh fruits and veggies, a little dairy or other protein and healthy fats, and you'll be fine.

why eat breakfast...and how

If you'd like a little more direction, use this guide to optimal serving sizes from WebMD.com and it'll be hard to overeat. Balance is the answer: use a little less of any one thing and you can keep piling on the flavors and textures.

- Apples, pears, oranges, bananas, tomatoes—any whole fruit: one medium piece equals a serving
- Strawberries, blueberries, raspberries: 1 cup
- Melon: 2 cups
- Dried fruit: ½ cup
- Vegetables: 1 cup (2 cups for leafy greens)
- Nuts: ¼ cup
- Cooked oatmeal: ¾ cup
- Skim milk, low-fat yogurt, low-fat cottage cheese, skim ricotta: 1 cup
- Reduced-fat cheese: 1 ounce
- Light cream cheese: 1 ounce
- Natural peanut butter: 1 tablespoon
- Canadian bacon or lean ham: 2 ounces
- Turkey bacon: 2 strips
- Smoked salmon: 1 ounce
- One egg

breakfast staples:

milk
& yogurt

Milk is just magical. Warmed, it will put you to sleep; cold, it will jump-start your day. Protein, calcium and vitamins A, B12 and D are just a few on its long list of health benefits.

The choices nowadays are mind-boggling. Cow's milk alone comes in fat-free (skim), 1% milk fat, 2% milk fat and whole. If the cows were fed on grass and raised without antibiotics or growth hormones, their milk is organic and the producers tout the additional omega-3 fatty acids you're ingesting.

If you're lactose intolerant or you're allergic to cow's milk, you can choose almond, coconut, rice or soy milk. Many of these are fortified with calcium and vitamin D, and you avoid the saturated fat and cholesterol in cow's milk.

Real buttermilk, the liquid left over after milk is churned into butter, is making a comeback across the country. Use the real deal if you have a trustworthy source for it, or the commercial variety that comes in liquid and powdered forms.

The popularity of yogurt has just exploded in the United States in recent years—a perfect example of everything old being new again. Long before anyone had the words to write out a grocery list, humans consumed fermented, semi-solid cultured milk. Any numbers of countries have tried to take credit for yogurt—who wouldn't? The most amenable of ingredients, yogurt—and the fermented milk drink, kefir—will only improve foods sweet or savory, hot or cold.

Doctors recommend three servings of milk, yogurt or cheese a day. Let's get to it!

soda fountain faves

soda fountain faves

I used to know a girl in college who was perpetually on a diet and whose breakfast consisted of a cigarette and a can of TaB®. I wouldn't recommend this. Instead, variations on soda fountain favorites will make breakfast fun, fast and usually healthy (as long as you use a light hand with the add-ons).

If you're planning to serve any of these for a party or to weekend guests, it's worth investing in classic soda fountain glassware: You can find banana boats, sundae dishes and soda fountain glasses at retroplanet.com.

Milkshakes in the morning make that first recommended glass of the day sweet. Blend a cup of milk or kefir (a type of liquid yogurt) with a scoop of frozen yogurt and a handful of fruit. Two cups of yogurt

soda fountain faves

blended with fruit is a popular Indian drink called lassi. (Smoothies get their own chapter later.) To get your caffeine boost, try equal amounts of coffee and milk with a scoop of chocolate frozen yogurt.

If you like a little "bubbly" upon awakening, wipe a wedge of fresh orange around the mouth of a 12-ounce soda fountain glass to flavor and wet it. Dip the rim in a saucer of sugar to coat. Pour in eight ounces of Orangina®. Drop in one scoop of blood orange sorbet. Garnish the glass with an orange slice.

Spoon three-quarters of a cup of hot oatmeal in a five-ounce sundae dish. Top with a generous scoop of your favorite yogurt. Sprinkle with dried cranberries and balance a good-looking walnut on top. (More about steel-cut oats and other whole grains later.)

Every early riser deserves a reward. A banana split isn't just for dessert anymore. Scoop three different flavors of your favorite frozen yogurt or sorbet into a banana boat. Place two halves of the banana, sliced lengthwise, on either side. Spoon blueberry and pineapple preserves on the right and left scoops. Garnish them all with chopped pecans. Drop a dollop of Greek yogurt on the middle scoop and finish with a section of clementine on top.

A piña colada parfait will transport you to a thatch-roofed bar on the pristine sands of some tropical isle. Spoon yogurt into a chilled rocks glass. Cover with pineapple preserves and sprinkle with coconut. Garnish the glass with a wedge of lime. Bottoms up!

breakfast staples:

oatmeal
& beyond

Have you tried steel-cut oats, a/k/a Irish oatmeal? They're more substantial than rolled oats since the whole, raw oats are chopped and left in pieces. They require more cooking time than rolled oats, about 20 minutes in all. Their nutty flavor is a complement to the usual sweet accompaniments of brown sugar, cinnamon, raisins and apples.

Amaranth, farro, millet, quinoa, teff and other nutrient-packed grains and seeds can be soaked and popped in the slow cooker the day before to save time in the morning. Top with any combination of coconut or almond milk, mango, blueberries, maple syrup, cream, bananas, coconut flakes, honey, dried cherries, dried cranberries, walnuts, sliced almonds, chia seeds, strawberries or preserves. You can even try savory add-ins, such as cheese, diced ham or crumbled sausage.

Try these and the days of white toast and home fries at your house are numbered!

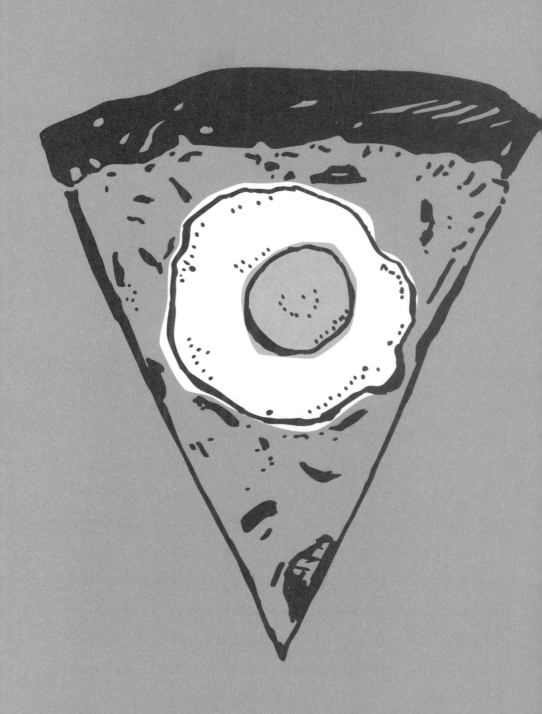

pizza for breakfast

Not the cold, congealed slice from last night. (Just last night? Are you sure?!) This is freshly made and lighter than the traditional pie. Just five inches across, it's a happy face waiting to happen.

Pizza dough can be frozen for up to three months, so you won't have to prepare this often, unless you're feeding a lot of people at once. These personal pies are really fun if you have overnight guests or if you're entertaining kids. Set up toppings in individual bowls for a make-your-own pizza bar. You can bake six at once on a regular baking sheet. Eat 'em with your hands; cartoons on TV optional.

The wonders of pizza really never cease. Kneading is a great outlet for your end-of-a-long-week/end aggression.

pizza dough

One packet active dry yeast

1 cup hot water, separated (approximately 100°F,

pretty much what comes out of your hot tap)

3 cups flour, and more for dusting

1 teaspoon salt

1 tablespoon olive oil

1. Mix all the yeast in ¼ cup of hot water. Set it aside for 10 minutes. Savor that yeasty smell and watch it bubble.

2. Combine flour and salt into a bowl. Make a well in the middle and pour the yeast mixture in, another ¾ cup of hot water and the olive oil. Mix until it holds together.

3. Turn onto a flour-dusted board, and knead for 6 to 8 minutes. You've got to put your back into it; push the dough away from you with the heels of your hands, fold it over, give it a quarter turn...same again until it's smooth and elastic.

4. Oil a big bowl and put the dough in, turn it over so the top is greased, and let it sit in a warm, quiet place for an hour and a half, until it's twice its size. Punch it down and divide into 8 pieces. Shape them into disks and wrap them individually in plastic wrap. Put these into a freezer bag.

pizza for breakfast

When you want pizza for breakfast, defrost a disk in your fridge overnight. The next morning, preheat the oven to 500°F, roll the dough to a 5-inch circle, brush with a little olive oil, top, lay it on a baking sheet dusted with cornmeal, and bake for 8 minutes.

Try a handful of mozzarella cheese as the base, add crumbled or sliced breakfast sausage, and a handful of chopped red pepper. Top with a little more mozz'.

Swirl salsa on the bare crust, top with corn, drained from the can or cut off the cob, chopped black olives and a handful of cheddar cheese.

Make a rim on your crust. Ladle on salsa, and break an egg on top. After it's baked, season with fresh cilantro.

Bake the oiled crust for 8 minutes; add cold smoked salmon, ¼ cup of sour cream, capers, fresh dill, and a spritz of lemon juice.

For a new twist on the BLT, chop up a tomato and toss with cooked bacon crumbles and a dollop of mayo. Top with arugula after it comes out of the oven.

Take a cue from popular cheese and fruit pairings, such as gorgonzola and grapes, gouda and strawberries or brie and apples, all with a drizzle of honey.

In the summer, the last thing you want to do is turn on your oven. Cut a "slice" of watermelon, drizzle with balsamic vinegar, and top with crumbled feta or goat cheese.

buttermilk pancakes... hold the syrup!

I love buttermilk pancakes, but I never seem to have maple syrup at home—neither the natural sweetness lovingly tapped from actual trees nor the fabricated kind that pours from a plastic likeness of a 19th-century cook. If you, too, find yourself syrup-less, don't let that stop you from enjoying these fluffy discs of old-fashioned goodness.

Making the batter requires some attention—I admit to mucking things up if I'm still half-asleep. My trick for getting the two mixtures combined in the right order is to say to myself,

> " Let's get you out of
> these wet things
> & into something dry. "

easy buttermilk pancakes

Makes 4 pancakes

¼ cup self-rising flour

½ tablespoon sugar

½ cup buttermilk

1 tablespoon beaten egg

½ tablespoon melted, cooled butter

1. Thoroughly mix the flour and sugar in a big bowl.

2. In a separate bowl, mix the buttermilk, egg and butter.

3. Make a well in the flour mixture and pour in the buttermilk mixture. Stir until just combined and don't mind the lumps.

4. Coat a hot frying pan with more butter and drop in small ladlefuls of batter—you can make two at a time or, if your pan's big enough, all four at once. (If the batter gets a little thick, use a dash of buttermilk to thin it.)

5. Cook until bubbles form on the top; flip and cook another minute or so.

buttermilk pancakes...hold the syrup!

The no-syrup twist is...wait for it...buttermilk pancake sandwiches! Messy, but totally worth it. Try any of the combinations suggested below or customize to your heart's delight.

You never have to eat or serve the same sandwich twice. It's easy to add anything to the batter in the ladle before you pour out a single pancake: flaked coconut, fresh blueberries, chopped dried apricots, even chives and other herbs—you name it. Then craft the center from fresh ingredients for a breakfast sandwich you won't feel guilty about enjoying.

sweet:

- Raspberry jam and peanut butter

- Chocolate syrup and chopped hazelnuts

- Half a banana, sliced, and Asian mandarin orange sauce (a sweet and tangy condiment available in the international food aisle of any supermarket)

savory:

- A slice of fresh tomato, a slab of fresh mozzarella, a few fresh basil leaves, olive oil and balsamic vinegar

- Ham and Cheddar with grainy brown mustard

- Thin-sliced smoked turkey, avocado slices and bacon

a short
digression
on a
1960s
breakfast

Pass right over this if you're nauseated by the nostalgia for the days of Tang® and freeze-dried coffee.

I grew up in 1960s suburbia. Breakfast Monday through Saturday was a bowl of Cocoa Krispies® or Lucky Charms®, doused with sugar and swimming in whole milk. Listening to the "snap, crackle, pop" or picking out the marshmallow shamrocks was fun. Slurping down that saccharine-sweet milk was heaven. If the milkman hadn't delivered yet, we'd douse the flakes in orange juice because God help you if you took the last of the milk before Mom made her first cup of coffee.

Sundays were somewhat easier on our teeth, though not our arteries. After church, Mom made my grandfather's beloved scrambled eggs, creamy curds improved by little melted blobs of American cheese. With them, we ate bacon and English muffins spread with margarine, a nod to heart health in those days.

On special occasions we got made-from-scratch French toast, which my mother prepared in her electric frying pan as my dad crushed ice for whiskey sours.

It was years before I encountered muesli, fresh papaya and steel-cut oatmeal, ingredients so exotic in America at that time as to be invisible. I love them all and use them regularly, but I still hanker for cereal, scrambled eggs with cheese, French toast, bacon. Don't we all? Let's just agree to eat them less often. On my parents' and grandparents' birthdays, I like to sit down to an old-school breakfast and remember the love they ladled out so generously.

breakfast staples:

breads & butters

The choice of breads and dairy and nut butters has grown exponentially in the last few years, particularly with the increase in gluten-free and allergy-free options.

Whatever type of bread you buy, make sure it says 100% whole grain on the label; if it's stone-ground, all the better. If you're buying peanut or another nut butter, the first item on the ingredient list should be peanuts or almonds or cashews or whatever. If you're buying a dairy butter, the first ingredient should be milk.

If that list is short and you can recognize and easily pronounce everything else in it, proceed to the check-out counter.

What about English muffins, croissants, pita bread, bagels, jellies, jams and that ubiquitous chocolate-hazelnut spread staring out so seductively from the shelves? Life would not be worth living without variety, so enjoy these within reason and turn your attention to taking on the world!

a toast!

Is there anything more inviting than toast? Perfectly browned warm bread is like a blank canvas: there's no end to the artistry once you start piling on fresh ingredients to taste.

Smørrebrød, Danish open-faced sandwiches usually served at lunchtime, are the inspiration for these quick-to-make, topless breakfast squares. These are as much about the look as they are the taste. Think contrast: white or yellow cheeses on dark bread; brightly colored jam on a pale slice. Make a pretty pattern with your fruit or vegetables. Add as much visual interest as you can with fresh herbs, drizzles, sea salt and fresh-ground pepper. Don't ignore texture: if the bread is whole grain, then you'll want something smooth on top, maybe with a little extra crunch from a light sprinkling of nuts. If the bread has an airy crumb, toppings with a little snap are perfect.

a toast!

Lightly toast one half of a pita. Spoon a quarter cup of ricotta on top. Dust it with chopped, lightly salted, shelled pistachios. Push green apple slices into the cheese. Drizzle with pomegranate molasses. The glass to raise? **Hot or iced mint tea**.

Toast a slice of whole grain bread. Spoon a quarter cup of plain Greek yogurt on top. Push fresh blueberries into the yogurt. Sprinkle with chopped hazelnuts and drizzle with honey. The glass to raise? **A cup of Greek coffee**.

Toast a slice of pumpernickel bread and spread thickly with herbed cheese. Arrange a half-dozen snow pea pods on top. The glass to raise? **Sparkling water with a slice of lemon**.

Toast a slice from a seeded loaf of semolina. Spoon a quarter cup of ricotta on it. Lay strips of roasted red peppers in oil on the cheese. Add pitted and sliced black olives. Sprinkle with sea salt. The glass to raise? **Fresh-squeezed orange juice**.

Toast a slice of sourdough and spread with hummus. Top with sliced avocado, fresh or roasted red pepper, and salt and pepper to taste The glass to raise? **Bellini**.

Brush a piece of whole wheat pita with olive oil, sprinkle with a liberal amount of za'atar spice and stick it in the toaster oven until it's crisp. Serve with hummus and labne for dipping. The glass to raise? **Pomegranate tea**.

Toast a slice of focaccia and spread with blue cheese. Top with

a toast!

sliced pears and a drizzle of honey. The glass to raise? **Pear nectar**.

What's better than one piece of toast? Two! The only possible verdict for the person who invented grilled cheese? Sainthood.

Ploughman's Lunch is a traditional British pub meal consisting of a hunk of rustic, crusty bread, a wedge of local cheese and Branston Pickle, a chunky, savory chutney. For breakfast, cut two thick slices of rustic, crusty bread; butter one side of each; swipe any savory chutney you like on the other sides; lay two slices of cheddar cheese on the chutney; press the chutney/cheese sides together, and grill. The glass to raise? **A mug of sparkling apple cider**.

When I was growing up, little kids regularly ate cream cheese and jelly sandwiches. Nothing wrong with spicing that up for adult palates, but no cutting off the crusts anymore! Butter two slices of raisin bread on one side of each. Spread cream cheese on the other sides. Add a generous amount of your favorite jam to the cheese; press the cheese/jam sides together, and grill. The glass to raise? **Cold, fresh milk**.

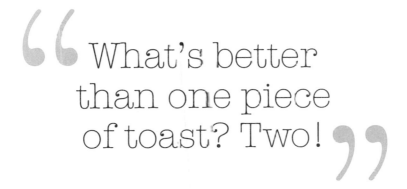

" What's better than one piece of toast? Two! "

Apple Mini-Pie

puff pastry...
it's classy!

Like a good set of pearls that makes any outfit—even skinny jeans—more elegant, puff pastry will turn breakfast into an event. Even if you're eating alone, treat yourself. Puff pastry tarts and turnovers take no time to make fresh and can be made ahead in a big batch, frozen, then defrosted and popped in the toaster oven on busy mornings.

Why keep this chic breakfast item to yourself? Invite friends and family to a leisurely breakfast or brunch. Let the champagne and fresh orange juice flow freely, pour café au lait into those fetching little bowls the French love to drink from, and debate the merits of "The Bicycle Thief" vs "Day for Night." Deliver a tray of these tarts to the table with a flourish and bask in the praise.

" Ooooh la la! "

small tarts

1. Preheat the oven to 400°F.

2. Gently roll out a defrosted sheet of puff pastry and cut out a rectangle about 4 by 5 inches.

3. Cut quarter-inch strips the length of each side of the rectangle. At this point, put the rectangle on baking parchment or a silicone mat. From painful personal experience, getting this off even a floured cutting board after you've crimped the edges turns a clean rectangle into a wacky amoeba shape...not so classy.

4. Brush the edges of the rectangle with water and press the strips onto the edges. Crimp them lightly with a fork.

5. Put in the fillings and then brush the tops of the crimped edges with an egg beaten with a tablespoon of water (that makes them glossy—spare no effort).

6. Bake for 15 minutes. Let them cool a moment, then dig in.

puff pastry: it's classy!

tart fillings:

Make egg salad filling to your taste with one hard-boiled egg. Sprinkle with the herb of your choice. It'll taste best if you season with abandon. Doesn't hurt to gild the lily with this one.

Spoon enough leftover mashed potatoes to put a fluffy bed down for two fully cooked sausages (Banquet® Brown-'N-Serve™ sausage links are the perfect length), sliced in half lengthwise. Tuck them in cut-side down and give it all a good twist of fresh-cracked pepper.

You can also mix sweet and savory by substituting a generous tablespoon of good-quality preserves for the mashed potatoes. Omit the twist of pepper; this is just delicious without any further ado.

try a turnover:

Turnovers are even easier than tarts. Give it a tropical twist by mixing in a bowl half a kiwi, peeled and chopped, with a generous tablespoon of drained, crushed pineapple, a handful of coconut and a pinch of brown sugar. Mix with just enough vanilla Greek yogurt to bind it all together. Cut a 5-inch square of pastry, turn the square so a corner is facing you, and brush edges with water. Spoon mixture onto bottom point of the square, leaving the edges exposed. Pull top half over filling. Crimp edges, brush the top with egg wash, and make two slits in the top. Bake for 15 minutes at 400°F.

puff pastry: it's classy!

What's one of the best things about Thanksgiving?! Pie for breakfast! Go all out and make a lattice-topped circular treat. You can share this if you like or eat it all yourself. I know what I'd do.

apple mini-pie

Half a baking apple cored, peeled and sliced

1 teaspoon each of sugar and cinnamon, mixed

Lemon juice

2 tablespoons apple jelly or other preserves, to taste

1. Toss apples with cinnamon sugar; sprinkle with lemon juice. Set aside.

2. Cut 2 circles 5 inches in diameter from a sheet of puff pastry. One is for the base of the pie. From the other, cut out the middle, leaving ½ inch on the outside.

3. Cut 6 quarter-inch strips 5 inches long.

4. Moisten the edge of the base with water, spoon the preserves and apple mixture into the middle.

5. Place the top over the filling and lightly crimp around the edge. Drop a couple of pats of butter on the apples. Place the first strip lightly across the middle and the second from top to bottom, in a cross shape. Weave your lattice as best you can and press down the edges. Brush the strips and edge with egg wash.

6. Bake for 20 minutes at 400°F.

puff pastry: it's classy!

Since puff pastry is pricey, we don't want to waste a scrap. Take that circle left over from the top of your apple pie, square it off and drop about six chunks of bittersweet chocolate on it. Swipe a little water on one end, roll into a cylinder, secure the end and the sides, and brush with egg wash. Take out of the 400°F oven after 15 minutes.

"Voilà!
Poor man's pain au chocolat (or, as the French would inevitably say, a poor excuse for pain au chocolat.
Let them sneer, it's sinfully good)."

washington
flapjacks

oregon
salmon hash

n. california
granola,
yogurt
& fruit

colorado
denver
omelette

s. california
cantaloupe &
cottage cheese

new mexico
huevos
rancheros

texas
breakfast
tacos

alaska
sourdough
pancakes

hawaii
loco moco

oklahoma
chicken fried
steak & waffles

U.S. breakfast
specialties what's your home state specialty?

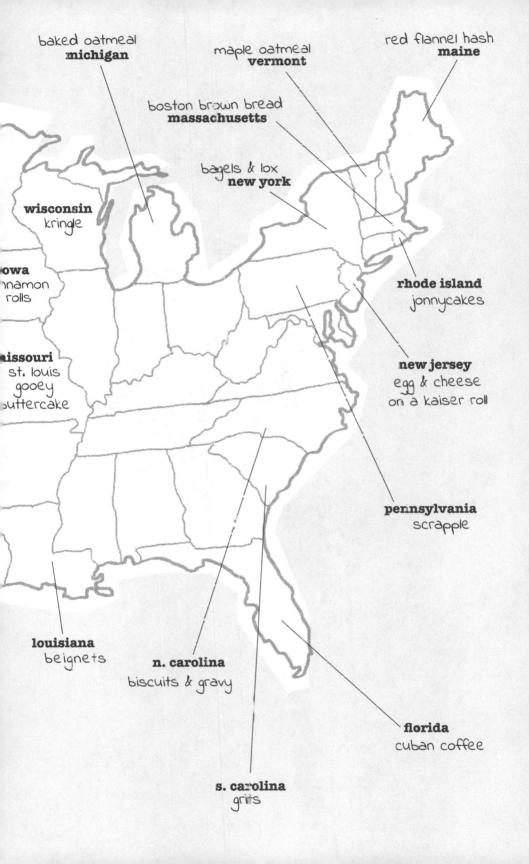

baked oatmeal
michigan

maple oatmeal
vermont

red flannel hash
maine

boston brown bread
massachusetts

bagels & lox
new york

wisconsin
kringle

owa
nnamon
rolls

rhode island
jonnycakes

missouri
st. louis
gooey
buttercake

new jersey
egg & cheese
on a kaiser roll

pennsylvania
scrapple

louisiana
beignets

n. carolina
biscuits & gravy

florida
cuban coffee

s. carolina
grits

breakfast
around
the world

spain

Breakfast = el desayuno

Greeting = "Buenos Dias!"

If you regularly ate dinner at 10 p.m., would you want a big breakfast? Spaniards enjoy a cup of *café con leche* or indulge in the sweet, piped and fried dough called *churros* dipped in hot chocolate. A savory alternative is *Pan con Tomate*, toast rubbed with garlic and fresh tomato and drizzled with olive oil. ¡*Buen provecho*!

mexico

Mexico's breakfast is influenced by many cultures. The Aztecs bequeathed modern Mexicans their unique-tasting chocolate, which they drink, when they're not drinking strong café, with water or milk, and spices. The French left them *bolillos*, delicious, crusty rolls. Spanish conquistadors christened the ancient corn disc eaten everywhere since time immemorial, tortilla. On that inviting edible plate, Mexicans put beans, chiles, tomatoes, cilantro, salsa, eggs...you name it. We love the idea of revving up your day this way so much, we've got a whole chapter on burritos for breakfast.

germany

Breakfast = Frühstück

Greeting = "Guten Morgen"

Germans love their smoked meats anytime—morning's no exception. The breakfast table is not complete without *Schinken* (ham) on a thick, buttered slice of sourdough bread or sandwiched in a buttered caraway seed roll. You'll also find soft-boiled eggs in the shell, preserves, honey and *Kaffee* (if it's served *mit Schlag*—with a dollop of whipped cream—look again, you've probably wandered into Austria).

denmark

Breakfast = morgenmad

Greeting = "God Morgen"

Do they eat Danish in Denmark? Yes, but they call it Weinerbrød, which translates as Viennese bread. These glorious, inventive fresh pastries are not made at home as often as they are bought in a bakery where they beckon from inside sparkling glass cases like precious stones in a jeweler's showroom. At home, it's cheese or jam on small round rolls or on sourdough rye bread with orange juice and pots and pots of coffee.

turkey

Breakfast = kahvaltı

Greeting = "Günaydin"

Turkey has always been a crossroads of East and West. The familiar and foreign mix in a bowl of clotted cream called *kaymak* with Turkish honey and in the traditional skillet dish *menemen*, scrambled eggs prepared with fresh tomato, onions, green pepper, cheese, oregano and mint. Pile either on oven-fresh bread and sip a small glass of black tea.

israel

Breakfast = aroḥet voker

Greeting = "Boker Tov"

You can thank Israeli pioneers for the tradition of a hearty breakfast: farming on a kibbutz in the early morning, the coolest part of the day, they worked up quite an appetite. They slaked it—still do—with hummus and baba ghanoush, olives, fresh vegetable salads, and the savory filled pastries called *bourekas*. Fresh fruit juice adds a sweet touch.

japan

Breakfast = choushoku

Greeting = "Ohayou," or the more formal "Ohayou Gozaimasu"

In a world as different from ours as Japan, you might feel completely upside down and backwards. Breakfast is a good example. Faced with bowls of steamed rice and miso soup, strips of dried seaweed and broiled fish, it'd be understandable to think you'd overslept by 12 hours. A rolled omelet will look more familiar. The elegance and calm of the food's presentation will convince you that confusion is sometimes the way to total peace of mind.

brazil

Breakfast = pequeno almoço

Greeting = "Bom Dia"

Brazilians dine lightly in the morning on nutrient-rich fresh fruits and their juices. Open-air markets sell guava, mango, and passion fruit, as well as the native acai berry, touted all over nowadays as a superfood. Strong coffee with milk and freshly-baked bread are other common items on most breakfast tables in this vast country with re-gional variations galore.

Breakfast = proinó

Greeting = "Kaliméra"

Ardent locavores, the Greeks' breakfast does not travel far to anyone's table. Individual, savory pies are popular, made with the cheese of the area, such as feta or kasseri. Sausages were recently on the hoof at neighboring farms and homemade preserves probably started with fruit from the trees outside the back door. Contrary to its name, the newly popular thick and tangy yogurt was not invented by the Greeks. They can claim the Olympic Games as their own, but not fermented milk.

Breakfast = zavtrak

Greeting = "Dobroye Utro"

Russians complement an easy, satisfying breakfast of rye bread and sliced sausage with black tea. On special occasions, particularly during a festival to commemorate the beginning of spring, home cooks will take the time to make *blini*. After a harsh Russian winter, the sight of these hot, golden disks, waiting for a variety of delicious sweet and savory fillings, must be very welcome indeed.

burritos for breakfast

How about starting your day with a little present of delicious goodness wrapped in more delicious goodness? An eight-inch whole wheat tortilla has the same 100 calories as a slice of whole wheat bread, and it makes a wonderful packet for what would otherwise require utensils or spill off your bread and make a mess.

Nowadays you have the option to make your tortilla fresh, as tortilla presses are widely available and affordable, or warm the ready-made wrap, in a microwave for 30 seconds. That makes it tastier and more flexible.

If your filling is solid or bound with melted cheese, you can just roll the tortilla. If it's loose and chunky, it's better to fold over the sides and roll the filling inside a packet.

burritos fillings

Scramble one egg with salt and pepper and the herbs/spices of your choice. Put a generous handful of Mexican-style shredded cheese on a "cold" tortilla. Top with the scrambled egg. Drizzle with chili sauce. Roll and microwave for 45 seconds. (If you're especially hungry, throw in any combination of black beans, salsa, sun-dried or diced tomatoes, avocado, onions, yogurt...you get the idea!)

Core and chop half an apple. Mix with a handful of walnuts, chopped celery, a handful of shelled edamame (perfect protein), and a tablespoon of mayonnaise. Microwave the tortilla for 30 seconds, spoon the Waldorf-style salad onto it, fold in the sides, and roll.

burritos for breakfast

Chop a little romaine lettuce, fresh tomato, cucumber and red onion Mix with a handful of feta cheese and a tablespoon of vinaigrette dressing. Encase in the tortilla and microwave for 45 seconds.

Or why not combine baked beans, grilled tomatoes, eggs and bacon or sausage in a warm tortilla for a portable English breakfast treat?!

Really, when it comes to breakfast burrito fillings, anything goes: grilled asparagus, ham and Gruyère or mozzarella; steamed broccoli and shredded cheddar; sautéed spinach and crumbled feta; mushrooms and creamy goat cheese; Nutella® and banana; figs, honey and ricotta.

"Let the good
times roll!"

breakfast staples:

eggs

If I were stranded on a desert island, what one food source would I want? A hen. Not for the one-time, undeniable pleasure of roasted legs, wings or breast, oh no. For the daily delight of fresh eggs. Nothing delivers protein, healthy fat, vitamins and minerals with so few calories as an egg. I'd treat that chicken like a queen.

Keeping chickens has become popular in recent years and one day, when I move to a place where the foxes don't roam, I might have a chance to show a laying hen my undying gratitude. Until then, I'll take the opportunity to buy my eggs at the local farmer's market. If you don't have a fresh supply, you can try the cage-free eggs at your local super-market, which also probably sells organic eggs from chickens that are antibiotic-free.

it

only

takes

1

egg

Cut a hefty slice out of the middle of a ripe tomato. Grill it on both sides in a little olive oil, season with salt, pepper and herbs to taste. Top with a poached egg.

Cut a thick round of cored green pepper horizontally, making sure it's not broken. Heat a swirl of olive oil in a frying pan. Place the pepper in the middle. Crack an egg inside and fry to your taste.

Line one hole of a muffin tin with a round slice of ham. Crack in an egg. Bake at 350°F for 20 minutes until the egg is set. Sprinkle with fresh chives, and there you have it—with apologies to Dr. Seuss—green eggs and ham!

Deviled eggs are divine. Still, I can't help but try to improve on their charms. Save that cooked yolk to garnish a bowl of fresh greens or warm potato salad and replace it with corned beef hash. If you're looking for all-the-protein and less-or-no cholesterol, fill the egg white with hummus, guacamole, pastina in pesto, caponata or tapenade.

Soft-boil an egg and slice off the top. Instead of toast cut into strips, dip cooked asparagus spears into the yolk.

Dip two slices of whole grain bread into one egg beaten with a scant ¼ cup of milk, a spoonful of sugar, a shake of salt and a ¼ teaspoon Cointreau or Grand Marnier. Fry them up and serve with a sprinkling of powdered sugar and fresh orange segments.

egg cozies

There's nothing sadder than a naked soft-boiled egg. Even in a pretty egg cup, that bald, fragile shell needs a warming topper, appropriately called a "cozy." Take a few minutes, a little felt, needle and thread, and your imagination to bring it some comfort.

Cut two pieces of felt, using the template below. When you've decorated one or both sides, sew up the round edge with a running stitch.

You could stitch this "cheep," black-on-white, pictured at left.

You can make a lady bug out of red and black felt, and a paper clip for the antennas (unbend the paper clip, bend it back into a "U" shape, wrap the two ends around a pencil and secure between the two sides at the bend in the middle.).

For a more whimsical topper, cut out a circle 4 inches in diameter of red felt, make four cuts almost to the center at 2 o'clock, 4 o'clock, 8 o'clock and 10 o'clock, and sew these cut sides together. You've made a little mushroom cap. Decorate with white felt polka dots.

Fit the cozy on your egg and you've done your good deed for the day (not to mention, keeping the egg warm for your eating pleasure).

Template

breakfast staples:

fruits &
vegetables

When it comes to fruits and vegetables, go bold and be adventurous. Head for the brightest, richest-colored ingredients for maximum nutritional value and to the most unfamiliar for the surprise factor. You never know what you might fall in love with!

If you try, as health professionals recommend, to eat nine servings of fruits and vegetables a day, you can keep the thrill alive by asking, "What'll I eat next?" And here's a mnemonic for remembering that recommended daily amount: there are nine letters in the word "vegetable."

Immigrants from around the world have brought with them their appetite for the fruits and vegetables of their homelands, which has introduced to us an amazing array of different things to try. It's not unusual for a supermarket these days to offer six different kinds of chiles, gnarly new root vegetables, and fruits as exotic as Buddha's hand. To delight your senses, visit a Latin American, Asian, Greek or Caribbean specialty market to buy dragon fruit, guava, persimmon, plantain, quince, star fruit, tamarind or tomatillo. Epicurious.com has a terrific visual guide to help you identify all these new choices.

Don't pass by the supermarket freezer section, either. Fruits and vegetables flash-frozen just after they're picked can be nutritionally more valuable than the pyramids of "fresh" ingredients that might've come off the vine or the branch weeks ago.

There's not much we eat for breakfast that can't be improved by a dose of Mother Nature's best medicine.

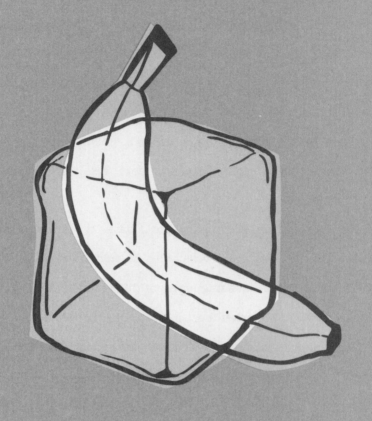

smoothies
1-2-3

Stopping at a commercial smoothie stand will set you back a few bucks. Save money and have it your way by stocking your freezer when you find an enticing fruit on sale.

Frozen fruit, rather than fresh fruit and ice, give smoothies a richer consistency and more intense fruit flavor. Bananas can go in the freezer skin and all; everything else will need washing; coring, peeling and seeding, if necessary; and cutting up before you lay the pieces on a cookie sheet. Allow for plenty of breathing room. After a couple of hours, they're ready to go into a container or freezer bag and into the freezer for up to 6 months.

Take a dozen pieces out up to half an hour before you make the smoothie to give your blender a break. You wouldn't want to break rocks first thing in the morning, either!

Smoothies don't need to be complicated. The best are as simple as 1,2,3.

1. Pour half a cup of juice into a blender (ideally, 100% fruit juice, but a tart fruit such as cranberries will have had some sweetener added).

2. Add a dozen pieces of frozen fruit.

3. Add a dash of flavoring, anything from pomegranate molasses to fresh ginger, peppermint extract to ground nutmeg.

Blend to your preferred consistency. It's not necessarily a breakfast replacement; it's a delicious infusion of a portion of the fiber, fructose (the natural sugar in fruit), vitamins and minerals we should eat every day. Add this to some source of protein and you'll feel full and be fully functional all morning long.

My Papa and me,
Chicago, Illinois

Even as a baby,
I was a little fuzzy
headed in the a.m.

My Nana and me,
Weston, Connecticut

breakfast like grandma(pa) used to make

While my grandmother was a terrific home cook, it was my grandfather, Papa, who excelled at scrambled eggs. He taught his technique to my mother and today, my brother, Papa's namesake, carries on the tradition. The comfort foods of our grandparents' era make a nice change when you want a slower, simpler start to the day.

individual bread pudding

Make an individual bread pudding by buttering one slice of cinnamon raisin bread and cutting it into cubes. Beat one egg with two tablespoons of sugar, add a quarter-cup of milk, and pour over the bread. Let that sit for 15 minutes, then pour into a buttered ramekin. Place the ramekin inside an 8 inch x8 inch pan. Pour water into the outer pan until it's three-quarters of the way up the ramekin. Bake for 35 minutes in a 350°F oven.

roasted fruit

Preheat the oven to 400°F. Toss half an apple and pear, cored and coarsely chopped, with a sprinkling of cinnamon and a spoonful of honey or maple syrup. Roast for 20 minutes on tin foil or a sheet pan until fruit is soft.

fruit crumbles

Preheat the oven to 425°F. Mix a medium-size bowl of hulled strawberries and picked-over blueberries with a quarter of a cup of brown sugar and a half-tablespoon of corn starch. Set aside. Mix a handful of chopped walnuts with a quarter-cup unbleached flour, a good shake of cinnamon, a good shake of salt and a generous pinch of brown sugar. Cut in chunks of cold butter until the topping looks like rough crumbs.

Divide the fruit mixture into three to four ramekins, making sure to use all the fruits' juice. Pack on the topping and bake for 20 minutes, until bubbly.

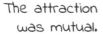

The attraction was mutual.

butterscotch
blast-off

butterscotch granola

It's tough to tuck a fried egg on toast or a pineapple parfait in your pocket for a midday snack, but granola will do the trick. It's a wonderful treat that has a million authors: everybody thinks his or her version is the best. This is called Butterscotch Blast-off for two reasons: it's a delicious handful of energy and a simple riff you can improvise on to suit your taste.

1. Preheat the oven to 325°F.

2. Combine one cup of old-fashioned rolled oats with half a cup of chopped nuts; add a good shake of salt and cinnamon. Mix well.

3. Boil a quarter-cup of honey and an eighth of a cup of canola oil for one minute and pour over the dry mixture. Mix well until every oat and nut is covered. Spread in a single layer on a baking sheet lined with baking parchment.

4. Bake at 325°F for 5 minutes; toss the oats and bake for another 8 minutes.

5. Cool completely; the mixture will crisp up. Break into pieces.

6. Add a handful each of butterscotch morsels and raisins.

It will keep in an air-tight container for one week (well, it should, but I've never known it to last that long).

hash browns:
new and improved

When it comes to nutritional value, potatoes get a bad rap, but that's because we do terrible (yet terribly delicious!) things to them. Before they're turned into French fries or slathered with butter, sour cream and bacon bits, they're low in calories, fat free and a great source of magnesium, potassium, vitamin C and vitamin B6.

hash browns: new & improved

Hash browns aren't always good for you, but they can be with this recipe that uses leftover potatoes. The nice thing about using leftovers to make hash browns is that they're not as watery as raw potatoes, so you won't have to drain or pat them dry after they're diced or shredded.

hash browns

1. Shred or dice baked or boiled potatoes. Low-starch varieties like Yukon gold and Russet work best. Keep the skin on if you want to boost your morning intake of vitamin C.

2. Preheat a cast iron skillet over medium or medium-high heat.

3. Add a teaspoon or so of coconut oil.

4. Once the oil is heated, distribute potatoes evenly in the pan then cook for 6 minutes or until the potatoes are crispy and golden brown on one side.

5. Flip the potatoes and cook until they're done.

6. Season with salt and pepper; serve with ketchup and hot sauce.

mix it up:

For variation, add any combination of red and green peppers, mushrooms, onions and sun-dried tomatoes during step 4. Boost the flavor by throwing in herbs like rosemary, thyme or dill right before they're finished cooking. Adding a bit of cheese when the potatoes are done won't kill you, especially if you choose a type with bold flavors. A little feta, sharp cheddar or Gruyère goes a long way.

breakfast
soups &
salads

You don't usually find soups and salads on the breakfast menus of diners and other classic breakfast places in the United States, but both are morning favorites in many parts of the world. Asians love to start the day with a rice porridge called *congee* or *jook*, as well as miso soup. All over the Mediterranean, people dive into a tray of fresh olives, tomatoes, cucumbers and more at first light. When eggs and bacon or toast and peanut butter get old, pull open the fridge's crisper drawer, reach into the freezer, and snip off a sprig of herbs to concoct something new and invigorating.

breakfast soups & salads

Let's build a soup pantry first. Keep a fresh supply of milk, buttermilk or kefir on hand and homemade chicken or vegetable stock in the fridge or in cans in the cupboard. Fresh or canned corn kernels, potatoes, carrots, celery and onion will add substance and flavor. If you love toast in the morning, croutons will satisfy the craving and help make soups (and salads, for that matter) more filling. Chives, parsley, basil, dill and mint for garnish are just a few herbs you can grow in a window box for that perfect finishing touch.

There's no better way to meet a chilly day than with a bellyful of hot soup.

Cut an "X" in the bottom of 1 medium-to-large fresh tomato and drop into boiling water for 2 minutes. Peel off its skin and chop. Put tomato in a pot with a good shake of basil, vigorous shakes of salt, a few grinds of black pepper and a pinch of sugar. Simmer for 5 to 10 minutes until the tomato softens and releases its liquid. Purée with a splash of heavy cream. Adjust seasonings and serve hot.

Fry a strip of bacon in a saucepan. Remove and crumble when cooled. In bacon fat, sauté a mixed cupful of chopped onions, green pepper, celery and potatoes for 5 minutes. Add a cup of milk. Simmer until potatoes are tender, 6 to 8 minutes. Add a handful of fresh or frozen corn kernels; heat through. Purée half the mixture, return to the pot, season to taste with salt and pepper. Serve with crumbled bacon.

The bright color of this soup will put a smile of your face on the dreariest of days. Wash and dice 2 medium carrots. Sauté a handful of onion

breakfast soups & salads

in butter, until soft. Add carrots, a cup of vegetable or chicken stock and ¼ cup of orange juice. Simmer until the carrot is soft. Purée with a splash of heavy cream and chopped fresh or dried dill to taste. Serve hot.

When the temperature threatens to soar, a chilled sweet or savory soup first thing in the morning will help you keep your cool. Make it the night before and leave it in the fridge overnight to chill.

Chop half a ripe avocado. Sprinkle with a good squeeze of fresh lemon. Pour a cup of kefir into the blender. Add the chopped avocado with a shake of salt and purée. Chill. Garnish with chopped parsley and a handful of chopped roasted almonds.

Wash and prepare a dozen strawberries. Pour a cup of cold heavy cream into the blender. Add the strawberries, a drizzle of honey or agave syrup and purée. Chill. Add a handful of picked-over fresh blueberries. Serve with a dollop of your favorite yogurt.

Salads are your first chance of the day to be creative. Thoroughly wash a few leaves of kale, chard or spinach and cut the tough stems out; chop. Add sections of clementine or mandarin oranges with a few rings of red onion. Throw in a handful of roughly chopped walnuts. Dress lightly with Dijon vinaigrette.

Wash a few leaves of red-leaf lettuce and chop. Lay on them, in a pretty arrangement, quarters of a hard-boiled egg, strips of fresh red and yellow peppers, strips of ham and strips of Swiss cheese. Dollop with a light French dressing.

the kitchen of your dreams

If space and budget were no object, what equipment would you own to make breakfast easier and more fun? Here's an A-to-Z look at upscale and whimsical utensils and appliances:

Apple Peeler/Corer (hand-cranked for one long peel; just like grandpa used to do it)

Bagel Cutter (a/k/a, if you've caught a finger in it, the "guillotine")

Bullit™ Blender (10 seconds to breakfast heaven)

Bread Box (if Donna Reed had one, why shouldn't you?)

Bread Knife (spend the dough; you don't want torn, squished slices)

Café au Lait Bowls (for breakfasting like Audrey Hepburn)

Cast Iron Skillet (doubles as a tool of self-defense)

Ebelskiver Pan and Turning Tools (bakers, you haven't lived until you've mastered ebelskivers)

Egg Cups (see page 55; eggs looks so cute all dolled up)

French Press (for breakfasting like Catherine Deneuve)

Grapefruit Spoon (useless and invaluable at the same time—great for kiwi, too!)

Griddle (for upper arms like Michelle Obama)

Honey Dipper (another useless keeper: you'll do one thing with it, but oh so perfectly)

Juicer (wow, the kids didn't need to go to college anyway)

Microwave Egg Cooker (because five minutes to boil water is too long)

Pancake Molds (The Mona Lisa? George Washington? No, Darth Vader™ and Big Bird!)

Pancake Pourer (a bowl and ladle is so yesterday)

Panini Press (see page 31, grilled cheese is not just for lunch and dinner anymore)

Programmable Coffee Maker (because who can make coffee until you've had coffee?)

Toaster (advertised as "smart;" maybe it'd finish the kids' homework for them)

Waffle Iron (why should the Belgians have all the fun?)

Whistling Teakettle
(what, you don't want the roar of a locomotive running through your kitchen first thing in the morning?)

Yogurt Maker (maybe you can dig up the one you used in the '70s)

Zester (life is just better with zest!)

There are innumerable ingenious fruit and vegetable preparers. You can cut bananas into perfectly equal slices; hull strawberries; pit a mango; core, slice and dice a pineapple. Look, Ma, no hands! But there's something about the mindfulness you can bring to preparing breakfast, with its fresh smells and stolen bites, in those quiet moments before the morning rush hour that will make it possibly the very best moment of your whole day.

you're
fueled
up....

knock 'em dead

credits

Illustrations on cover, 02, 04, 06, 08, 26, 40, 50, 56, 66, 69: iStock
Illustrations on 16, 20, 46, 58, 72: Denis Kohler
Photography on 10, 28: iStock Photography on 14, 32: Thinkstock

sources

Why Eat Breakfast? And How!

http://www.webmd.com/food-recipes/features/healthy-breakfast-ideas-and-recipes

Breakfast Around the World

Germany:
www.germanfoods.org

Spain:
www.whatvalencia.com

Mexico:
http://www.mrbreakfast.com/w_mexico.asp

Japan:
http://web-japan.org/kidsweb/faq/life01.html

Greece:
www.olivetomato.com

Denmark:
http://www.copenhagenet.dk/cph-eating.htm

Turkey:
http://foodieinternational.com/the-best-turkish-breakfast-in-istanbul.html

http://www.seriouseats.com/2012/11/snapshots-from-istanbul-turkish-breakfast-is-awesome.html

Israel:
http://www.seriouseats.com/2012/07/serious-entertaining-israeli-breakfast-recipes.html

Brazil:
http://kblog.lunchboxbunch.com/2008/08/breakfast-around-world-list.html

Russia:
http://gorussia.about.com/od/food_and_drink_in_russia/a/russian_breakfast.htm

http://russiapedia.rt.com/of-russian-origin/blini/Israel:
www.seriouseats.com/2012/07/serious-entertaining-israeli-breakfast-recipes.html

acknowledgments

It's 6 a.m., a quiet start to what promises to be a beautiful spring day. It's the perfect time to reflect on the help, support and cheering-on I received from family and friends throughout the writing of this book.

Thanks to my husband, Chuck, for his steady good nature and to Grace for her eagerness to see what each new day will bring.

Thanks to my family for their honest appraisal of these ideas.

Thanks to Christine Zika, whose invaluable suggestions as she read and reread the manuscript improved it so much.

Thanks to Rachel Corbett for her contributions and cheerful encouragement.

Thanks to Cheryl Meglio for her eagle copyeditor's eye.

Thanks to Denis Kohler for his artistic talent, imagination and patience as we both ventured into new territory.

Thanks to Lisa Ferris and Claire Giobbe for leading us through this territory to a happy place.

the end

Americans welcomed the "Toastmaster" pop-up toaster into their kitchens, marveling at just how easy burning sliced bread can be.

1926

1921

Was it in Harry's Bar in Paris where the bartender invented the Bloody Mary, or did he first concoct it later in 1934 in New York City? Who cares?!

1952

The "Today" show debuts on NBC-TV with its first host, Dave Garroway. Those who write for the back of cereal boxes suffer a sharp drop in royalties.

TODAY